Recipes from New Mexico, Back to Simplicity from the Land of Enchantment

Acknowledgements and Dedications

I would like to dedicate this book to my three children, Michelle, Sabrina, and Crystal Chavez. I truly hope that they will express interest in learning to prepare the food of their culture. Also, that they may pass down to their children these very delicious recipes from mychildhood.

I Love You Always, MOM

Maria Phyllis Chavez

I would also like to thank my God Daughter, Katherine Perez. She helped me with the construction of this book. I really appreciated her help!

And last but not least, I don't want to forget my beautiful Mother, Rita Sedillo, who taught me to cook most of these recipes, with her witty words ofwisdom.

ISBN-13: 978-0692721865
Copyright 2009
www.MariaPhyllis.com

Table of Contents

Easy Salsa	7
Potatoes with Ground Beef, Onions and Green Chili	9
Red Chili Pod Sauce	11
Carne Adobada (Marinated Meat In Red Chili) 13	13
Chilaquiles	15
Chili Beans	17
Tacos	19
Tamales	21
Chili Con Queso (Green Chili Cheese Sauce)	25
Chili Rellenos (Stuffed Green Chili Peppers)	27
Caldillo	29
Spanish Rice	31
Stuffed Sopapillas	33
Pinto Beans with Spinach	35
Fast Calabasitas (Zucchini)	37
New Mexico Green Chili Stew	39
Huevos Rancheros (Ranch Style Eggs)	41
Powdered Red Chili Sauce with Meat	43
Pinto Beans	45
Posole	47
Spanish Salad	49
Flat Enchiladas	51
Rolled Red Chili Enchiladas	53
Flour Tortillas	55
Sopapillas	57
Saucy Rice	59
Biscochitos	61
Sweet Rice Pudding	63
Sopa (Bread Pudding)	65
Eggnog	67
Atole	69
Empanadas	71
Pumpkin Empanadas	72
Pie Crust	73
Bean Tostadas	75

Measurements & Translations

T.	=	Tablespoon
t.	=	teaspoon
c.	=	cup
lb.	=	pound
0z.	=	ounces
Qt.	=	quart
Med.	=	medium
Pkg.	=	package

Most of these recipes are for 4 to 6 servings except for the desserts and drinks.

Easy Salsa

28 Oz. can diced Tomatoes
1 t. Vinegar
2-4 Jalapenos (diced)
1 med. Onion (diced)
1 Clove Garlic (chopped well)
½ t. Salt
½ c. chopped Cilantro
½ Stalk-Green Onions chopped
(only use half of green part and all of white part) Pinch Pepper
Juice of one Lemon

Mix all ingredients together. Store in refrigerator, covered, for a couple of hours to blend flavors.

This type of Salsa is usually preferred on Tostadas, but can also have many uses. May be served with eggs for breakfast, or on Tacos. The uses are endless.

Potatoes with Ground Beef, Onions and Green Chili

1	lb. Ground Beef
4	Potatoes (diced)
1	Onion (diced)
¼	t. Garlic Powder
¼	c. chopped New Mexico Green Chili Pinch of Pepper

Salt to taste

On medium heat, brown ground beef in a medium frying pan. Empty most of grease, except for 2 T. Add potatoes and salt. Cover and fry until tender. Add onion, green chili and garlic powder. Stir, add a pinch of pepper, and fry about 3 more minutes.

You may use this for filling in burritos or just scoop them up with pieces of tortillas. This may also be served with fried Eggs in the morning or as a side dish for dinner. May also be used for Taco filling.

Red Chili Pod Sauce

20	Dry Red New Mexico Chili Pods
1	Clove Garlic
1	t. Salt Water

Rinse chili pods in cold water. Break off stems and discard. Transfer to 3 quart saucepan. Add enough water to cover chili and boil for about 5 minutes to soften. Discard water.
Add all ingredients into a 48-ounce blender. Fill about half the blender with fresh, cold water. Blend or Puree for about 5 minutes. If too thick, add a little more water. In a medium sized frying pan, add about 1 t. olive oil. Add chili and simmer for about 4 minutes.

This chili can be used for Enchiladas, Burritos, or Huevos Rancheros, or even just by itself on anything you want it on.

These chili pods can be bought in most grocery stores. Just make sure they are New Mexico Chili pods for a more distinct flavor.

Carne Adobada

Marinated Meat In Red Chili

2-3   lbs. Pork, boneless Ribs or Rump Roast Red Chili Marinate (recipe below)

Pierce meat a few times, so marinate will absorb, and add meat to red chili marinate. Let sit overnight or for about 6 hours in refrigerator. Place meat in a baking dish without the extra marinate and bake in the oven at 325 degrees for about 3-4 hours or until meat falls apart. You may also cook the meat in a crock pot for 8 -10 hours on a low setting.

This meat is used as a main dish or can also be used for Burritos. Fried potatoes make a great side dish as well as refried beans.

Red Chili Marinate

- 20   Dry Red Chili Pods
- 3   c. Water
- 2   t. Salt
- 2   Garlic Cloves

Rinse chili pods in cold water. Break stems off and discard. On medium heat, boil in water in a 3 quart sauce pan for about 5 minutes to soften. Discard water and place chili in a 48-ounce blender and fill with 3
c. of fresh, cold water. Add salt and garlic. Blend and puree about 5 minutes.

Chilaquiles

Corn tortilla pieces in chili sauce

Chili pod sauce recipe (recipe in this book)
- 1 dozen Corn Tortillas (cut in small bite size pieces)
- ½ medium Onion
- 1 cup grated Jack Cheese
- 4 T. Oil

In large frying pan, fry tortilla pieces in oil until very crispy. Add onion and fry a little longer until onion is translucent. Add chili. Simmer about 5 minutes. Sprinkle grated cheese on top. Cover and cook until cheese melts. If you want to serve in a nice oven proof platter, you may place chili mixture in platter first, add cheese and bake until cheese melts.

Chili Beans

1   16oz bag dry whole Pinto Beans cooked in 3 qt. sauce pan (recipe in this book)
½   c. Red Chili (either the chili pods or powdered chili-both work well)
1- 2   lbs Ground Beef
1   t. Salt
½   c. diced Onion

In 3 qt sauce pan, brown ground beef. Add onions. Cook until onions are translucent. Drain grease and add to beans. Cover and simmer for about 15 minutes.

Serve with warm tortillas or crackers. You may add lemon juice and shredded cheese to taste. May also sprinkle with chopped Cilantro.

Tacos

1	dozen Taco Shells
12	oz. Grated Cheese (preferably Colby or Jack)
1	t. ground Cumin
3	tomatoes (diced)
½	t. Garlic Powder
½	head of shredded lettuce
½	med. diced Onion
1	lb lean ground Beef
1	t. red New Mexico Chili Powder
½	t. Pepper
1	t. Salt

Preparing the Meat

Add spices to meat and brown in a medium size skillet. Cover and simmer about 5 minutes, stirring occasionally. Drain grease. Add approximately 2 T. meat sauce in each taco shell. Top with grated Colby or Jack Cheese, diced tomatoes and lettuce. You may also use fresh spinach or cabbage as an alternate for lettuce.

Preparing the Taco Shells

If you are using store bought shells, bake empty shells in oven at 350* for about 3 minutes before filling. This makes them taste better. To make homemade shells, fold corn tortillas in half with tongs, holding both ends together at the top. Dip the bottom fold into hot fat or oil until very stiff. Fin- ish by frying each side of corn tortilla until stiff. This method will keep the bottom part of shell open and will make it easier to fill.

Tamales

2-3 lb. Rump Roast or other meat that will shred after cooking
1 t. Salt
½ t. Garlic Powder
3 t. Salt
3 T. Baking Powder
½ t. Pepper
1 recipe Red Chili Sauce
1 c. Shortening or Lard
½ bag Masa Harina
(this is a special type of flour used for making tamales)
1 bag Corn Husks Liquid from boiled meat

Preparing the Meat

Add meat to a 3 quart sauce pan. Add enough water to cover meat. Add 1 t. salt and ½ t. pepper. Simmer for about 3 hours or until meat practically falls apart. Remove meat from sauce pan and save broth. Shred meat completely with two forks.

Combine Red Chili Sauce and meat in a clean saucepan. Add
1 t. salt and ½ t. garlic powder to chili. Simmer for about 3 more minutes. Place into a bowl and set aside.

Preparing the Dough

2	lbs or 1/2 bag Masa Harina
1	T. Baking Powder
2	t. Salt
1	cup Shortening or Lard liquid from boiled meat

In a large bowl, combine all dry ingredients . Mix well with a whisk. Add liquid from meat and mix well, adding liquid until consistency of dough feels sticky or is of spreading consistency. If all liquid is used you may continue adding water to dough.

Preparing the Corn Husks

Fill sink with water. Separate corn husks one by one and soak in water for about 10 minutes or until pliable. Place on towel and pat to dry. Place meat, dough, and husks on table, giving yourself enough room to work.

Making the Tamales

Get one corn husk, add about 1 tablespoon dough and spread thinly to about 3/4 of the husk, leaving the bottom or pointed side doughless. Add 1 tablespoon of meat filling to middle of the husk over dough. Fold left side of husk over meat, then fold the right side over the left side. Finally, fold the bottom side up. You may tie tamale with strings made with leftover husks if you want it to stay secured.

Cooking the Tamales

When cooking Tamales, use a 6 or 10 quart sauce pan. Line the bottom of your sauce pan with crinkled aluminum foil or left over corn husks. Fill bottom of sauce pan with 2 inches of water. Stand tamales on top of foil or corn husks, leaving
the open side facing up. Try not to let tamales stand in water. Cover the top of tamales with extra corn husks, then cover sauce pan. Let tamales steam for about 2 hours on very
low heat. Do not let water evaporate. Keep adding water if
needed. Corn husks will peel easily from tamale when fully cooked.

Individuals will peel corn husks from tamales when served. May serve with red chili sauce over tamales.

Chili Con Queso Green Chili Cheese Sauce

¼	c. Flour
2	c. whole Milk
½	c. Margarine
¼	t. Garlic
½	t. Salt
½	c. Onion (diced)
16	oz. Velveeta Cheese (cubed)
3	New Mexico Green Chilis (chopped)

In a medium sized saucepan, melt margarine on medium heat. Add onion and stir until translucent. Add chili and stir. Add flour and stir. Add milk, slowly stirring constantly.

Simmer until thickened. Add garlic and salt and stir. Add cheese and stir until completely melted. If too thick, add a little more milk. Serve with tortilla chips.

This recipe may also be used in different types of Macaroni and cheese recipes.

Because this recipe has flour, a sediment will form on top when cooling. Remove this with a spatula and you will be able to reheat over and over again.

Chili Rellenos
Stuffed Green Chili Peppers

8-10 Hatch Green Chili Peppers
½   c. diced Onion
½   t. Baking Powder
½   t. Salt
2   T. sifted Flour
3   Eggs, separated
2   c. grated Cheese (preferably Jack) Oil to fry

Roast chilis in oven until brown or almost black. Remove chilis from oven and lay on damp dish towel and cover them completely for about two minutes. This will allow chili to peel easier. Peel chili, being careful not to break the skins. Cut a slit length wise on each chili pepper. Remove most of the seeds, but leave the stem in tact. Separate egg yolks from egg whites and beat egg whites until stiff peaks form. Beat egg yolks in separate bowl, then add sifted flour, baking
powder and salt to egg yolk mixture. Fold yolk mixture into egg whites.

Dip chili in mixture one at a time and deep fry on medium heat until golden brown. Align on cookie sheet and let chili cool to the touch before filling. Find the cut you made in your chili before frying it. Open up and fill with 2t. of grated cheese and ½ t. diced onion. Bake in a 350* oven until cheese melts. Serve in platter and drizzle with red chili sauce.

Suggestions: Serve with refried beans, Spanish rice, and rolled enchiladas, or tamales.

Caldillo
(Potato Soup)

1	Onion (sliced)
1-2	lbs. lean Ground Beef
5	diced potatoes (big pieces)
2	8 oz. cans tomato sauce
1	whole New Mexico green Chili
4	cans water (use same can from tomato sauce to measure)

Salt and Pepper to taste, do not go easy on the pepper as this is what makes the dish more flavorful

On medium heat, brown ground beef in a sauce pan. Add onion, stirring constantly until it is translucent. Add potatoes and stir well. Add tomato sauce and stir while adding water, salt and pepper. Bring to a boil, cover and simmer for about 45 minutes or until potatoes are tender. You may leave the chili in or remove it when fully cooked.

Spanish Rice

1	c. long grain Rice
1	T. Oil
½	Medium Onion (diced)
½	t. ground Cumin
1	t. Salt
1	8 oz. can Tomato Sauce
3	c. Water (approximately)

On medium heat, add oil, rice and cumin to medium frying pan and stir constantly until lightly browned. Add onion and stir about one minute, then add tomato sauce and stir. Add water and salt and stir well. Bring to a boil, then cover and simmer for about 20 minutes, or until all liquid is absorbed. Do not stir. To check if liquid is absorbed, stick a fork into rice, moving it away from the edge of pan. If liquid is ab- sorbed, then rice should be fully cooked.

Stuffed Sopapillas

Sopapillas -   (recipe in this book)

Cut a slit on one side of each Sopapilla Open and fill with about:

2	T. red Chili Sauce with meat
2	T. refried Beans
2	T. grated Jack Cheese
2	T. chopped Lettuce
2	T. diced Tomato

Serve with a side dish, such as spanish rice, refried beans, or calabasitas. You may also get creative with these and add any type of meat, such as diced chicken or steak. You may also eliminate the red chili and use salsa instead.

Pinto Beans with Spinach

4	T. Oil
½	Onion (diced)
¾	c. Fresh Spinach
2-3	c. whole cooked Pinto Beans without liquid (recipe in this book)

Salt and Pepper to taste

On medium heat, fry pinto beans in oil. for about five minutes, stirring occasionally. Add salt and pepper. Add onions and one more T. oil. Fry until onions are translucent. Add spinach and fry for about 3 more minutes.

This was considered a Lenten food for Catholic New Mexicans. Since we cannot eat meat on Friday's during the Lenten season, this was a good source of protein.

Fast Calabasitas (Zucchini)

3	Zucchini Squash (diced)
1	15 oz. Can whole kernel Corn (drained)
1	med. Onion (diced)
2	T. oil
2	New Mexico green chili's (chopped) Salt and Pepper to taste

On medium heat, add oil to frying pan and fry all ingredients together. Cover and simmer for about 5 minutes. You may add ground beef at the beginning of this recipe if you would like to make it a main dish instead of a side dish, just eliminate the oil and drain ground beef to about 1 t. of its own grease, add the rest of ingredients and simmer.

New Mexico Green Chili Stew

8	New Mexico green Chili's(roasted and peeled)
½	Onion (diced)
1	t. Garlic powder
1	lb. Ground Beef or round steak cut in very small pieces
1	Potato (peeled and diced)
4	cups Water (approx.)
1	diced Tomato

Salt and Pepper to taste

Add garlic powder to green chili and chop finely. Set aside. On medium heat, brown meat in a frying pan or skillet. If using ground beef, drain grease, if using steak, add about 1
t. oil, just enough to fry steak. Add onions and potato and fry for about 1 minute, stirring constantly. Add green chili and water and stir. Then stir in salt and pepper, adding tomato afterwards. Bring to a boil and simmer for about 3-5 minutes if using ground beef, or until potatoes are tender. If using steak, simmer for about 10 minutes, or until meat is tender.

Huevos Rancheros Ranch Style Eggs

4	oz. Jack Cheese
8	corn tortillas
4	eggs
¼	c. Oil
2	c. red Chili sauce

Heat chili in saucepan. In a medium frying pan, add oil and fry tortillas on medium heat. Make sure tortillas are soft, as they need to be in and out of the oil quickly. Using tongs, Dip each tortilla in the chili and align individually on a cookie sheet.
Fry eggs in oil in separate frying pan.
Place one fried egg on top of each tortilla. Cover the egg with about 1 T chili. Dip 4 more tortillas in chili and place one on top of each egg. Add about 1 or 2 more T chili on top of each tortilla. Top each with grated cheese. You may also add another fried egg on top of the last tortilla if desired. Finally, bake in 350* oven, just until cheese melts.

Powdered Red Chili Sauce with Meat

¼   c. Powdered New Mexico Red Chili
1   lb Lean Ground Beef or Round Steak cut in pieces*
1   t. Garlic Powder
1   t. Salt
¼   c. Flour (this is approximate) May use more or less as you master making this chili
2 ½   c. Water (again this is approximate)

In skillet, brown meat on medium heat. Add flour and stir for 1 minute. Do not drain grease. Add chili and stir. Almost immediately afterwards, add 1 c. water, stirring constantly. When thickened, add 1 ½ c. water. Bring to a boil. Lower heat and add garlic and salt. Simmer for about 5 minutes. You may add a little more water if the mixture is too thick.

This Chili may be used in Enchiladas, Huevos Rancheros, or as a side dish. Will also be a great addition to Burritos.

*If using Round Steak, you will need to use about 2 T. oil when browning , as this will help Chili to thicken.

Pinto Beans
(Homemade)

2	c. dry Pinto Beans	½	med Onion (cut in half)
1	T. Olive Oil	1	clove Garlic
1½	t. Salt		Water

Clean beans by spreading them on a table and removing all bad beans* or little rocks that might have been in the pack- age. Place beans in colander and rinse well with water. In a 3 quart sauce pan, add water about ¾ full. Add beans, onion, salt, olive oil, and whole garlic clove. Bring to a boil and simmer for about 3 hours until beans are very soft. Do not let beans run out of water. If needed, keep adding water
at the same amount it had from starting. Remove onion and
garlic and discard.

When fully cooked, these beans can then be made into refried beans by adding another 2 T. oil to a frying pan. Add enough beans with only enough liquid to make the right consistency. With practice, you will eventually learn what the best consistency for your taste is. On medium heat, mash beans with a potato masher, and simmer for about 3 or 4 minutes. If desired, add about ½ c. grated Jack cheese over beans and cover until cheese is melted.

*A pinto bean is not usually edible if it is dark in color or if it is shriveled.

Posole

(Hominy Soup)

2	lbs. Pork or Beef cut in small pieces
1	t. salt
2	29 oz. cans of Hominy
2	T. New Mexico red Chili Powder
1	diced Onion
1	clove Garlic (chopped)
1	bunch Cilantro (chopped) Water

Lemon wedges

Fill a 3 quart sauce pan ½ full with water. Add meat, then bring to a boil. Add salt and garlic and stir. Simmer for about 1 hour, or until tender. Add chili powder, then cover and simmer for another 10 minutes. Add can of Hominy, including liquid. Simmer another 5 minutes.

Place the onion, lemon wedges and cilantro in serving bowls. Each individual will use as much of these ingredients as they want. Usually, about a teaspoon of onion and ½ teaspoon of cilantro with lemon juice of one wedge is usually sufficient.

Hint- If fat or any sediment forms on top of meat while simmering, you should skim it off. You may also start off with a piece of meat that has not been cut or shred. This may be done after you finish cooking.

Serve posole with warm corn or flour Tortillas.

Spanish Salad

In med. size bowl:
½	head chopped Lettuce	½	c sliced Carrots
1	bunch sliced Radishes	½	diced Cucumber
¼	c. Croutons	1	c. diced Jicama
1	c. Spanish Olives	¼	c. Bacon bits
¼	c. grated Cheese (preferably jack or colby)		Salsa

Mix all ingredients together except for the salsa. Individuals can pour the amount of salsa they wish on their salad which will be used as a dressing.

Salsa

In blender:
2-3	Jalapeno peppers	2	cans Tomato sauce
½	med. Onion (cut in two)	1	clove Garlic
½	t. Salt	¼	c. Water
1	T. Lemon	¼	t. Pepper

Blend for about 2 minutes. Then add ¼ c. chopped fresh Cilantro and stir with a spoon.

Flat Enchiladas

Originally made like this in NewMexico

1	dozen Corn Tortillas
10	oz. grated Jack Cheese
1	med. diced Onion
1	recipe Red Chili Pod Sauce with or without meat

Fry all tortillas in hot oil. Just in and out of oil, they need to be soft and pliable. Dip about 4 tortillas in chili and place individually in a casserole dish or cookie sheet. Top each with about 2 T. chili sauce. Sprinkle each with about ½ t. onion and about 1 T. grated cheese. Top each with another dipped chili tortilla and repeat the process with the onion and cheese
layering 1 more time ending with the cheese. Bake 3 minutes
at about 350*

For the side dishes, try refried Beans and Spanish Rice.

If you do not wish to fry tortillas, dip the tortillas in red chili sauce before arranging the layers and bake, covered, for about 20 minutes instead of 3 minutes in the final stage.

Rolled Red Chili Enchiladas

12	Corn Tortillas
4	c. grated Jack Cheese
½	med. diced Onion
1	recipe Red Chili Pod sauce (in this book)
1	lb Ground Beef (optional)

Brown ground beef in medium skillet. Add all the chili. Simmer for a couple of minutes. In another frying pan, fry corn tortillas soft in hot oil. Dip tortillas one at a time in chili and lay flat in a cookie sheet one tortilla at a time, having about 3 or 4 laid in cookie sheet at one time until finished.
Add about 1 T. grated cheese and ½ t. diced onion to each tortilla. Roll tortillas and start aligning them on another cookie sheet until all are done. Add about 1 c. chili to the top of the enchiladas, and sprinkle about 1 c. grated cheese. Cover with aluminum foil and bake for 20 minutes at 350*.

Always cover enchiladas when baking, as meat will dry out and will not look very appetizing. Also, you may use the powdered Red chili recipe instead of the chili pod sauce.

Flour Tortillas

3	c. Flour
2	t. Baking Powder
2	t. Salt
¼	c. Shortening
2	c. Water (approximate)

In a big bowl, mix flour, baking powder and salt. Add shortening and mix well. Add enough water to make a soft
dough. Knead enough to where dough is no longer sticky, adding a little more flour if too sticky or, a little more water if too dry. Make into balls and cover with a dish towel so
dough will not dry. With a rolling pin, roll out to about 8 – 10 inch circles, depending on your preference. Cook on griddle over stove, on medium heat, turning once to cook on both sides until dough is cooked and tortilla is lightly browned.
Place in a clean dish towel, stacking until all tortillas are cooked, making sure tortillas are completely covered.

Roll tortillas very thin if planning to use for burritos. If using for just table tortillas, leave them thicker. When cooled, store covered or in a plastic zip lock bag in refrigerator. Do not worry if your tortillas do not turn out perfectly round, as my Mother would say, "they are not going in rolling".

Sopapillas

- 3   c. Flour
- 2   t. Baking powder
- 1   t. Salt
- 3   T. Shortening
- 1   c. Water (approximate) Oil for deep frying

Mix flour, baking powder and salt. Add 3 T. shortening. Knead with warm water until dough can be handled. If dough is too sticky, add more flour, and if dough is too dry, add more water. Make 6 or 7 balls with dough. Spread to about
¼ inch thick with rolling pin. Cut in 4 triangles with a knife.
In deep cast iron skillet, deep fry each triangle in very hot oil until puffy, about 2 at a time, turning once to fry on both sides. Should be golden brown. Place on big bowl that is lined with paper towels.

May be used in place of bread, but are great as a des- sert drizzled with honey. May also be stuffed with beans, cheese, lettuce, and tomato. Just cut a slit on one side of Sopapilla to fill.

You may use your own variations as they are endless.

Saucy Rice

¼	t. Pepper
1	t. Salt
1	T. Oil
2	c. long grain Rice
2	8 oz. cans Tomato Sauce
½	med. diced Onion
¼	t. Garlic powder Water

On medium heat, mix rice with oil and fry for about 2 minutes. Add onion and fry until translucent, stirring constantly until rice is lightly browned. Add garlic powder, salt, and pepper while stirring continuously. Add tomato sauce and using the empty can, add about six 8oz. cans of water. Bring to a boil, and then simmer until rice is
tender, stirring occasionally. Mixture should have consistency of soup. May add a little more garlic powder for additional taste.

This is not like traditional Spanish Rice. This is a soupier version of Spanish Rice, which was one of my favorites when I was growing up. Simple, yet delicious.

Biscochitos
(Spanish style sugar cookies)

1½	c. Lard or Shortening	4	c. Flour
2	T. Cinnamon	¼	t. ground Clove
¼	t. Salt	1½	c. Sugar
2	Egg Yolks	1	T. Anise seed
1	c. water*		

In medium size bowl, cream sugar and shortening or lard. Add egg yolks. In separate bowl, mix flour, cinnamon, clove, and salt. Sift this into shortening mixture. Add anise seed and mix well. Add water.
Knead until mixture sticks together. Sprinkle flour to countertop or board as needed to prevent dough from sticking. Sprinkle flour on rolling pin as well. Divide dough into balls and roll each ball about 1/4 inch thick, then cut with cookie cutters. Dip each cookie in cinnamon sugar on one side before placing on ungreased cookie sheet. Bake at 375* for 10 to 12 minutes or until lightly browned. Makes about
3-4 dozen cookies.

Preparing Cinnamon Sugar

Mix 1 c. Sugar with 2 T Cinnamon. You may choose to re-dip cookies in the cinnamon sugar after they come out of the oven.

Originally these cookies were made with lard instead of shortening. They are even more delicious when made with lard, but less fatten- ing when made with shortening. These cookies were always made during the Christmas season. They were always served to visitors with coffee or hot chocolate.

Try making variations by using sweet vermouth or juice in place of water, but the first time you make them, I suggest using water. Though not traditional, you may also add colored sprinkles if you have children.

Sweet Rice Pudding

2   c. long grain Rice
2   c. Evaporated Milk

In 3 qt. saucepan, boil Rice in water until tender. Drain liquid and blend together rice and evaporated milk and set aside.

In separate bowl, mix:

¼   c. Flour
3   Egg Yolks (save egg whites to use later)
2   c. fresh Milk

Beat with whisk until well blended. Pour in Rice and Milk mixture.

In 3 qt saucepan, add the mixture with ¾ c. sugar. Simmer, stirring occasionally, for about 10 minutes. In separate bowl, beat 3 Egg Whites until they peak. Fold in to Rice mixture.
Sprinkle Cinnamon on top.

Sopa (Bread Pudding)
AKA-Capirotada

1	loaf sliced Bread (approx.)
1	c. Raisins
½	c. white Sugar
½	c. brown Sugar
2	T. Cinnamon
3	T. pine Nuts or Pecans Water

Cheese (sliced)
1   20 oz. can crushed Pineapple (do not drain)

Toast the bread in a cookie sheet in the oven (about 400*). Add about 5c. water to a med. sauce pan. Add raisins, sugars, cinnamon, and pineapple. Bring to a boil and simmer until raisins are plump. About 5 minutes. Layer toast in an oven baking dish. (Rectangular) Make sure they are all touching. Add slice cheese to each bread. Add about a cup of raisin mixture over layer of toast. Sprinkle a couple t. pine nuts or pecans over all. Repeat layers a couple of more times, ending in liquid and more nuts. Make sure toast is completely absorbed in liquid. Cover and bake at 350* about 30 minutes. Use only the amount of toast you need to make even layers and enough sliced cheese to place on each bread.

This recipe was usually made during the time of the Lenten season. It was used as a dessert but sometimes can be used as a main dish.

Eggnog

3   c. Milk
1   Egg
2   Cinnamon Sticks (broken in half) Sugar to taste
Ground cinnamon

Bring milk and cinnamon sticks to a boil in very low heat, stirring frequently, which will be about a 10 minute process. Remove from heat. Remove cinnamon sticks from milk by straining into a small pitcher. Beat egg well in a separate bowl and pour into milk mixture, beating with a whisk the entire time. After you finish pouring in egg, beat about 15 seconds longer. Add sugar to taste or you may also use about 1 T. honey to taste.

Pour eggnog into cups. Sprinkle with ground cinnamon on top. Add one cinnamon stick to each cup for decoration.

We drank this in the morning, if you didn't have time for a
full breakfast or if your were on the run. Serve with buttered French toast or just toast.

Atole
Blue Cornmeal Drink

2	c. Water
½	c. Blue Toasted Cornmeal (comes in cellophane bag)
2	T. Evaporated Milk

In 1 quart sauce pan, simmer water and cornmeal until thickened. Add more water until it is of drinking consistency, a little thicker than hot chocolate. Simmer about 3 minutes. Pour into cups. Add about 2 T. Evaporated Milk to each c. of Atole with salt and pepper totaste.

Some people also drink this with sugar instead of salt. I prefer it with salt. May also use honey to sweeten instead of sugar.

This was used originally for stomach upsets, but believed
to be very nourishing by our New Mexico Native Americans, and also Native New Mexicans. My Mother drank this all her life, mostly when she had an upset stomach. She lived until she was 94 years young.

Empanadas

(Individual Fruit Pies)

Pie Crust (recipe on page 72) canned fruit filling (any fruit) Cinnamon Sugar (recipe on page 60) Milk

Roll pie crust. Cut with a large round cookie cutter. Add 1 tablespoon fruit filling to each pie circle. Fold over to meet ends. Use water to seal, then fork to finish sealing. Brush milk on top of each empanada. Sprinkle cinnamon sugar on top of each. Bake at 350* or until golden brown. (about 20 minutes)

Pumpkin Empanadas

1	15 oz. can Pumpkin	1¾	t. Pumpkin Spice
½	c. Sugar		
2	T. Milk		
1	beaten Egg		
1	pie crust recipe		

Add beaten egg to milk and beat again. Add the rest of ingredients and mix well. Roll pie crust. Cut with a large round cookie cutter. Add 1 T. pumpkin mixture to each round cut out. Fold over to meet ends. Use water to seal, then fork to finish sealing. Brush milk on top of each empanada. Sprinkle cinnamon sugar on top of each. Bake at 350* or until golden brown. (about 20 minutes)

Pie Crust

3	c. sifted flour
1	t. Salt
1	c. Shortening
¾	c. water

Sift flour and salt. Add shortening. Cut into mixture with a fork or whisk until mixed well. Add water and knead only until everything sticks together. Use extra flour on board or counter and also rolling pin to keep from sticking.

In the olden days, this recipe was made with dehydrated fruit. Fruit was sliced and stored on roofs of houses on top of gunny sacks until completely dried with the sun. Later they were rehydrated, when they were ready to make empanadas or some other dried fruit dish.

Bean Tostadas

½ dozen Corn Tortillas
3 c. refried Beans (recipe in this book)
1 10 oz. pkg. grated Jack Cheese
2 c. chopped lettuce
2 diced tomatoes

Fry tortillas in 1/2 c. oil until crispy. Spread each tortilla with a thin layer of beans. Top with cheese, lettuce and tomato in this order. Serve Salsa on the side for pouring over tostadas. Spanish rice and Calabasitas are good side dishes.

Hint- you may use store bought tostada shells, but if you want to make them yourself, an easy way is to spread the soft corn tortillas on paper towels and keep turning them occasionally so they do not curl up. This process will take a few hours. Then you may fry them. They will be very crisp and more delicious than just frying them without this process.

About the Author

Maria Phyllis Chavez / Sedillo was born in Clovis, New Mexico. Her family left Clovis when she was about three years old. They moved to Albuquerque and was raised there until her Marriage in 1968. Although currently single, she now resides in Phoenix, Arizona, where she continued her education in Medical Billing and Coding, now an M.B.S. (Medical Billing Specialist) . She has always loved cooking and baking. Also a Cake
Decorator, she also baked and sold many cakes of different occasions throughout her life, including wedding cakes. She wants to preserve and hand down her Mother's recipes and the recipes she loved to her Children, Grandchildren, Family, and Friends.

TRADITIONAL AND SIMPLE RECIPES FROM ONE FAMILY

www.ingramcontent.com/pod-product-compliance
Lightning Source LLC
Chambersburg PA
CBHW061047090426
42740CB00002B/65